BECOMING YOUR OWN BOSS

Part 1

THE BUSINESS IDEA

Maxine J. Lovell

Riverflow Writers Publishing

Copyrighted Material

Copyright © 2020 by Maxine J Lovell

Becoming Your Own Boss Part 1
The Business Idea

Part of a Three Book Series

Published by Riverflow Writers

First published in the United Kingdom 2020

ISBN: 9798556607040

Edited by Daniel Lovell
Proofread by Michael Lovell
Images https://pixabay.com

All rights reserved. No part of this publication may be reproduced, stored in a retrieval system, or transmitted by any means, electronic, mechanical, photocopying or otherwise, without the prior written permission of the publisher. The only exception is brief quotations in printed reviews.

TABLE OF CONTENTS

INTRODUCTION	3
THE NATURE OF AN ENTREPRENEUR	5
MOTIVES FUELLING ASPIRATION	9
GENERATING BUSINESS IDEAS	15
THE RESEARCH PROCESS	24
NARROWING DOWN IDEAS	34
BUSINESS VIABILITY	44
THE BUSINESS ENVIRONMENT	57
FINAL THOUGHTS & ADDITIONAL INFORMATION	69

INTRODUCTION

Have you ever had a business idea that excites you, but haven't taken the first step to turn it into reality? Maybe you think about it constantly, but don't know how or where to start.

Or perhaps you're still in the brainstorming phase, with a desire to launch your own business but without a clear direction.

If this resonates with you, this book is your roadmap to transforming your ideas into actionable steps, guiding you toward becoming your own boss and building the business you've always dreamed of.

I've been where you are, filled with the desire to start a business but unsure how to move forward. I'd talk about it, plan for it, but progress was slow. Life's distractions and daily demands often took priority, and I used them as an excuse for not taking action.

But I eventually realised that ideas alone don't build businesses, action does. And the sooner you move from talking to doing, the sooner you'll see results. If you're reading this, it means you're ready to take that leap, and I'm here to help you make it happen.

In this book, we'll dive into practical strategies and tools to help you generate, evaluate, and refine your business ideas. Through hands-on exercises and insightful examples, you'll learn how to transform a vague concept into a solid, viable business.

To get the most out of this journey, make sure to:

- Engage actively with all the exercises and activities.
- Conduct thorough market research for your product or service.
- Apply everything you've learned to your own business idea.

I've seen too many people read business books, get inspired, but fail to take action. Without execution, knowledge is just information, it's the application that turns it into results.

By the end of this book, you'll be equipped with the tools and mindset to confidently take the next step toward becoming your own boss. Let's get started on building the business you've always wanted.

THE NATURE OF AN ENTREPRENEUR

An entrepreneur is someone who possesses the right mindset, a relentless drive, and the courage to take calculated risks. At the core of entrepreneurship is the desire for self-sufficiency and autonomy, the freedom to make your own decisions, without being bound by the constraints of a corporate or bureaucratic system.

While the path of entrepreneurship is undoubtedly rewarding, it's not without its challenges. The road to building a successful business often requires grit, resilience, and the ability to face uncertainty head-on. The journey can be particularly difficult in the early stages, as the financial rewards may not be immediate, and life's circumstances can often make it harder to fully commit the time and effort required to make your business a success.

This reality leads many to choose the stability of traditional employment over the volatility of self-employment. However, if you're anything like me, you'll constantly seek ways to break free from the employee mindset because you're dissatisfied with being controlled by someone else's agenda.

My Journey to Entrepreneurship

From the age of 13, I had a vision for my life. However, despite my aspirations, I didn't achieve the grades I needed to pursue my desired career in college. This setback led me to a different path, and I ended up working as a hospital laboratory assistant for a year.

It was during this time that I realised the conventional career path wasn't for me. I couldn't shake the feeling that I wanted to be my own boss, inspired by watching my grandmother successfully run her own restaurant business.

My first real business venture came when I seized the opportunity presented by the **Enterprise Allowance Scheme**, introduced by Prime Minister Margaret Thatcher in the late 1980s. The scheme aimed to encourage the unemployed to start their own businesses by providing £40 per week in funding and offering enterprise training.

I launched a children's clothing business, purchasing items wholesale and selling them to parents at local playgroups, through friends and family, and even from my home. This model was simple and effective, I hosted party plans where I could showcase my products, while also exploring the opportunity to sell children's books as an additional revenue stream.

Unfortunately, the Enterprise Allowance Scheme only provided support for one year, and my business didn't survive beyond that period. I quickly became discouraged and, in hindsight, lacked the perseverance to weather the early-stage struggles. So, I pivoted and decided to pursue a degree in business, believing it would provide me with the knowledge to eventually launch my own successful venture.

After graduating, I transitioned into teaching and became a business and management lecturer. I enjoyed the role to some extent, especially after receiving positive feedback from students who I tutored outside of class. Their encouragement, combined with support from my professors, led me to secure a teaching position at a local university and college.

While lecturing was rewarding in its own right, I never felt truly fulfilled. I found myself hopping from one teaching job to another, all the while dreaming of entrepreneurship. Eventually, I left the education sector to pursue my original goal of becoming my own boss. Yet, even then, I struggled to take concrete steps in that direction. Instead, I ended up working in the housing sector, not because I was passionate about it, but because it was the only available option at the time. Despite this, I continued to take on freelance work as an online tutor, always seeking ways to transition out of employment and into self-employment.

My experiences in various sectors provided invaluable skills, but they couldn't satisfy my entrepreneurial itch. The bureaucratic nature of the workplace stifled my creativity and innovation. I realised, I could only truly thrive if I was running my own business, where I could make my own decisions, be agile, and ultimately pursue the freedom that comes with self-employment.

Is Entrepreneurship Right for You?

Becoming your own boss isn't for everyone. It requires unwavering commitment, a strong work ethic, and a readiness to face challenges head-on. You may need to make significant sacrifices, working long hours, dealing with uncertainty, and possibly enduring sleepless nights.

But if you're able to push through the tough times and stay focused on your end goal, the rewards can be extraordinary. The satisfaction of building something of your own, making independent decisions, and creating long-term success is what drives entrepreneurs to keep going, even when the going gets tough.

If you're ready to take that leap, to work harder than you ever have before, and to embrace the rollercoaster that is entrepreneurship, then you're on the right path. And though the road is challenging, if you remain dedicated and adaptable, you'll eventually reap the rewards of your hard work and commitment.

MOTIVES FUELLING ASPIRATIONS

Before embarking on the journey to become your own boss, it's crucial to understand your *why*. Your 'why' is the underlying reason driving your decision to take the leap into entrepreneurship. It's this purpose that will sustain you during the inevitable challenges and setbacks you'll face along the way. Without a clear understanding of your 'why', it's easy to lose motivation, stray off course, and ultimately abandon your venture when things get tough.

Defining your motives is the first step toward creating a successful business. By engaging in a self-reflection process, you'll gain clarity about the deeper values and aspirations that fuel your ambition. This clarity will empower you to make intentional decisions, overcome obstacles, and stay committed to your goals.

The following list outlines some common reasons entrepreneurs pursue their own businesses. These examples should help you identify your own 'why', the foundation of your business venture:

1. **Desire for Autonomy**: You've always wanted to work for yourself, make your own decisions, and be in control of your professional destiny. Now feels like the right time to make that leap.

2. **Better Work-Life Balance**: You want the flexibility to design your own schedule and prioritise personal time, creating a life that's more aligned with your values and aspirations.

3. **Passion Turned Profession**: You're eager to turn a hobby, skill, or passion into a thriving business that not only brings you joy but allows you to earn a living doing what you love.

4. **Identifying a Market Gap**: You've spotted a unique business opportunity or recognised a gap in the market, and you have a product or service that meets that demand.

5. **Financial Independence and Growth**: You're motivated by the potential for increased earnings, and you see entrepreneurship as a path to financial freedom and a better quality of life.

6. **Creating Impact**: You're driven by the desire to make a positive impact on your community, industry, or the world. You want to solve problems and contribute to meaningful change.

7. **Legacy Building**: You aspire to build something lasting that can provide value beyond your lifetime, whether that's a family business, a social enterprise, or an innovative product that reshapes an industry.

The Importance of Defining Your 'Why'

When you know your why, you have a powerful, emotional connection to your business that will carry you through both triumphs and challenges. Understanding why you're pursuing entrepreneurship will guide your decisions, help you stay grounded, and enable you to measure your success beyond financial gains.

Moreover, your 'why' serves as your north star. In moments of doubt or uncertainty, it's your 'why' that will reignite your drive and focus. It will allow you to stay true to your values and ensure that you're building a business that's aligned with your long-term vision.

Next Steps: Defining Your Personal 'Why'

Now that you understand common entrepreneurial motivations, it's time to dive deeper into your own. This exercise will help you define your personal reasons for starting a business and solidify your vision for your entrepreneurial journey.

Task: Identify Your Own 'Why'

1. **Reflect on Your Values**: Think about what matters most to you, what drives you, excites you, and gives you purpose. Consider aspects of your life that you want to improve or that inspire you to take action.

2. **List Your Top Motivations**: Use the list above as a guide but personalise it. Are you driven by financial freedom, autonomy, or a deep passion for a specific cause? What are the unique factors that make entrepreneurship appealing to you?

3. **Consider the Bigger Picture**: Beyond your personal motivations, consider how your business aligns with your broader goals. Do you hope to create a lasting legacy? Solve a problem in your industry? Help others in a meaningful way?

4. **Visualise Your Success**: Imagine your life after achieving your entrepreneurial goals. What does success look like to you? What kind of business have you built, and what impact has it had on your life and the lives of others?

5. **Write It Down**: Once you've completed this reflection, write down your personal 'why' statement. This statement should clearly articulate your core motivations and serve as a reminder of what you're working towards when times get tough.

Additional Insights for Entrepreneurs

While defining your 'why' is a powerful first step, it's important to remember that entrepreneurship is a multifaceted journey. As you prepare to build your business, keep the following points in mind:

1. **Set Clear and Achievable Goals**: Your 'why' is the foundation, but turning your vision into reality requires actionable, measurable goals. Break your business objectives into smaller, manageable tasks to stay focused and make consistent progress.

2. **Understand the Challenges**: Entrepreneurship is not a smooth road. Be prepared for setbacks, unexpected expenses, and periods of doubt. Your 'why' will help you stay resilient during difficult times, but a solid business plan and contingency strategies will be your safety net.

3. **Seek Mentorship and Support**: No entrepreneur is an island. Surround yourself with advisors, mentors, or like-minded individuals who can offer guidance, share experiences, and provide emotional support.

4. **Adapt and Evolve**: The business landscape is constantly shifting. Being adaptable and open to change is essential for long-term success. As you grow your business, keep refining your 'why' to reflect new insights, lessons learned, and evolving goals.

5. **Celebrate Progress**: Don't wait for the end goal to celebrate. Acknowledge milestones along the way, whether it's landing your first customer, completing a business milestone, or simply maintaining consistency in your efforts.

With a clear understanding of your why, you're not only setting the foundation for your business, but also equipping yourself with the mindset needed for success. As you move forward, remember that every challenge is an opportunity to learn, adapt, and grow. Keep your vision in mind and stay focused on the long-term impact you aim to achieve.

HOW TO GENERATE BUSINESS IDEAS
A Comprehensive Approach for Entrepreneurs

Starting a business begins with one fundamental step: generating a business idea. But how do you find that one idea that has the potential to become a successful business? How do you assess whether your idea can be turned into a viable venture? These are the two key questions every entrepreneur needs to answer before embarking on the journey of building a business.

Generating ideas and transforming them into real businesses requires both creative thinking and strategic analysis. The process of ideation involves tapping into both internal and external factors, leveraging your skills, and analysing market opportunities. By applying specific techniques, you can unearth a wealth of business ideas you might never have considered.

In this section, we'll dive deep into two powerful techniques: **The Scanning Technique** and **The Brainstorming Technique**. Together, these methods will guide you in recognising viable opportunities and refining your ideas to meet market needs. Let's explore them in more detail.

1. The Scanning Technique: Tapping into Your Potential and Market Demand

The scanning technique is about looking at both **internal** and **external** factors to identify potential business ideas. It focuses on:

Internal factors: Your personal skills, experiences, hobbies, and passions.

External factors: Opportunities within the marketplace or unmet needs in society.

This dual approach ensures that the business idea you choose is both feasible and aligned with your unique strengths. By scanning your environment, you may discover opportunities you never considered. Below are 10 areas you can focus on to generate ideas:

1. Talents

Look at your natural talents or acquired skills. What are you good at? This could be anything from problem-solving, communication, design, coding, writing, or even manual craftsmanship. Talents often form the foundation for a business that is both sustainable and enjoyable because they stem from your inherent strengths.

Example: A person with a natural ability for drawing or painting could start a custom artwork business, offering bespoke portraits or mural designs to homes, offices, and commercial spaces.

2. Hobbies

Many successful businesses start as hobbies. The key is to assess whether turning your hobby into a business will bring you joy or drain your enthusiasm. While some hobbies may lose their charm when monetised, others can be highly profitable.

Example: Someone passionate about baking could turn a hobby into a cake-making business, offering customised cakes for events or opening a small café specialising in baked goods. Another example is my uncle, who turned his love for Latin and Afro-Cuban dance into a thriving dance instruction business.

3. Experience / Career

Your career background is a goldmine for generating business ideas. Think about the expertise you've gained over the years, including any leadership or technical skills. Your professional experiences can give you a head start in understanding your industry, market needs, and how to structure your business.

Example: An experienced delivery driver might consider starting their own logistics or distribution service, utilising their first-hand knowledge of the industry.

4. Meeting a Local Need

Business ideas often arise when you spot a gap in your local community. Look for unmet needs or underserved markets in your area. By providing products or services that address these needs, you can build a loyal customer base.

Example: If you notice that pet owners in your area travel far to buy supplies, opening a local pet shop or offering a pet supply delivery service could fill an existing gap.

5. Things You're Passionate About

Passion fuels perseverance and helps keep your business afloat during tough times. What are you deeply passionate about, whether it's fitness, sustainability, fashion, or technology? Consider how your passion could solve a problem or meet a demand.

Example: A passionate animal lover might open a pet grooming service that doubles as an extension of a pet shop, offering both products and services that pet owners need.

6. Solutions to Problems

Businesses that solve problems tend to thrive, as customers are always looking for solutions to their challenges. The key is to identify pain points in everyday life or specific industries and figure out how to address them.

Example: A property investor could focus on solving the housing shortage by developing affordable rental properties, creating both social impact and financial returns.

7. Money-Saving Ideas

In a world driven by cost-cutting, a business model that helps customers save money is often highly valued. Explore areas like financial services, technology solutions, or products that reduce consumer spending over time.

Example: A financial advisor could develop a service that helps individuals save money on insurance premiums, mortgages, or energy bills by offering expert comparisons and advice.

8. Simplifying Practices

Think about everyday tasks or processes that can be made easier or more efficient. Many successful businesses have emerged from simplifying complex systems.

Example: The invention of the selfie sticks revolutionised photography by enabling people to take group photos without needing a third party. Such innovations often create new business opportunities in unexpected ways.

9. Gaps in the Marketplace

Sometimes, businesses succeed simply by offering something that is missing. If you can identify a gap in the market, you might be able to create a business that directly addresses that need.

Example: Airbnb identified a gap in the hospitality industry by offering budget-friendly, peer-to-peer accommodation options, creating a multi-billion-dollar business.

10. Improving Existing Business Models

Innovating on existing business models can lead to massive success. This is particularly true if you can find a way to make an existing service or product more efficient, affordable, or accessible.

Example: Uber and Lyft took the traditional taxi model and reimagined it through a smartphone app, creating a convenient and cost-effective solution for consumers.

2. The Brainstorming Technique: Refining Your Ideas

While the scanning technique helps you generate a broad range of ideas, the brainstorming technique helps you refine those ideas into actionable business plans. It's a creative, problem-solving tool that encourages both individual and group input to shape business concepts.

Individual Brainstorming

When brainstorming individually, focus on three critical areas:

1. **Types of Businesses That Exist:** Study existing business models and evaluate why they succeed or fail. Are there any that you could improve upon or innovate? This exercise will help you understand different business types, and which ones might suit your skills.

2. **What Attracts Others to These Businesses:** Reflect on why certain businesses appeal to you and others. This could be due to their customer service, innovative products, or unique value propositions. Understanding these elements will help you design a business that attracts your target audience.

3. **Wants and Needs:** Consider the wants and needs of your local community, friends, family, or even yourself. Are there any specific demands in your area that are unmet? Can these be turned into a profitable business idea?

By examining these areas, you'll develop a clearer picture of which business ideas are worth pursuing.

Group Brainstorming

While individual brainstorming is valuable, brainstorming with a group can provide a wealth of diverse ideas and insights. When collaborating with others, make sure you include people who share similar values and are passionate about the entrepreneurial process. Group brainstorming will help you see angles you may have missed and provide instant feedback on your ideas.

Diagramming Your Ideas: Use visual aids like mind maps or diagrams to expand on your ideas. For example, if your main business idea is based on "Experience in the Property Market," you can branch out to secondary ideas like property management, real estate investment, or property maintenance.

By involving others in the process and mapping out your ideas, you'll be able to focus on the most viable options.

Final Thoughts: Moving from Idea to Execution

Once you have a solid business idea, it's time to take action. **Research the market** to ensure there's demand, **create a business plan**, and **test your idea** through small-scale experiments. Don't be afraid to pivot or adjust based on feedback and changing market conditions.

Remember, generating a business idea is just the beginning. Execution, persistence, and adaptability will determine whether your idea becomes a thriving business. Keep scanning for opportunities, brainstorming innovative solutions, and continuously refining your approach.

Exercise: Your Business Idea

Now it's time for you to apply what you've learned. Using the **Scanning Technique**, generate at least three potential business ideas based on your talents, hobbies, experiences, or market gaps. Then, refine your ideas using the **Brainstorming Technique**, either individually or in a group, and decide which one you're most excited to pursue.

This is your first step toward entrepreneurship, take it with confidence, and let the journey begin!

THE RESEARCH PROCESS
Laying the Foundation for a Successful Business

As an entrepreneur eager to start your own business, one of the most important steps you'll take is to ensure that your idea is not only viable but also strategically positioned to succeed in the marketplace. In this section, we will delve into the research process that will guide you in assessing your business idea's potential, understanding your target audience, and positioning your business for success.

Why Research Matters

Conducting thorough research is crucial to gaining a deeper understanding of the business landscape you're about to enter. It serves as the foundation for making informed decisions that will shape your strategy, operations, and marketing. At this stage, research will help you:

1. **Validate Your Idea**: Ensure that your business concept has a strong chance of success by understanding market demand, customer preferences, and competitor dynamics.

2. **Identify Market Gaps**: Find opportunities where consumer needs are unmet or where you can offer something unique that sets your business apart.

3. **Evaluate Competitor Strategies**: Analyse what your competitors are doing well and where they may be lacking, so you can differentiate your offering and exploit market weaknesses.

4. **Determine Feasibility**: Assess whether your business is financially and operationally viable in the context of consumer demand and competitive forces.

5. **Refine Your Product or Service**: Improve your offerings by gathering feedback on product features, pricing, and other key elements that influence customer decision-making.

The Research Process: Key Steps to Take

1. Consumer Research: Understanding Your Audience

Your customers are the heart of your business. Knowing who they are, what they need, and how they make purchasing decisions will allow you to craft a more compelling offer. To conduct consumer research, consider the following methods:

Surveys and Questionnaires: Gather direct feedback on customer preferences, pain points, and purchasing behaviour.

Focus Groups: Use small groups of potential customers to discuss your product and gain in-depth insights.

Product Testing: Offer prototypes or beta versions to a select group to assess how well your product meets their needs.

Key Insights from Consumer Research:

Your research should answer these critical questions:

Viability: Does your business have the potential to thrive based on consumer interest and demand?

Target Market: Who are your ideal customers in terms of demographics, location, and consumers' behaviour? Do they have specific needs that your product or service can fulfil?

Sales Channels: Where will you sell your products? Will you operate from a physical store, through an e-commerce platform, or a combination of both?

Foot Traffic/Online Traffic: If you are considering a physical store, is there enough foot traffic to sustain your business? For online businesses, assess website traffic and e-commerce trends.

Brand Awareness: How will you create awareness and drive traffic to your business? Consider digital marketing, word-of-mouth, and local advertising.

Customer Retention: What strategies will you use to retain customers and encourage repeat purchases? This could include loyalty programs, excellent customer service, or high-quality products.

Promises and Guarantees: What unique selling propositions (USPs) can you offer? Examples include fast delivery, money-back guarantees, 24/7 customer support, or a price-match policy.

2. **Competitor Research: Knowing Your Competition**

Understanding your competitors is essential for positioning your business. Researching the strengths, weaknesses, and strategies of similar businesses will help you find your competitive edge.

Competitor Research Questions to Consider:

1. **Who Are Your Competitors?** Create a list of at least 5 businesses that directly or indirectly compete with you.

2. **What Are Their Sales Channels?** Do they have a physical store, an online presence, or both? How does their sales model align with your target audience's preferences?

3. **How Are Their Offerings Similar or Different?** Examine their product or service in terms of features, pricing, quality, and customer service.

4. **What Are Their Strengths?** What do customers praise about them? Is it the product quality, affordability, brand reputation, or customer service?

5. **What Are Their Weaknesses?** What are the gaps or areas where they fall short? Is it poor customer service, a lack of innovation, or limited product variety?

6. **What Strategies Are They Using to Attract Customers?** How do they market themselves? Are they using digital ads, social media, influencer partnerships, or traditional marketing methods?

7. **What's Their Pricing Strategy?** Are they positioned as a premium brand, or do they focus on low-cost solutions? Is there room for you to disrupt their pricing structure?

3. **Market Analysis and Identifying Opportunities**

Once you've completed your consumer and competitor research, you'll need to analyse the data to determine the market potential for your business. This includes:

Market Trends: Are there emerging trends that could benefit your business, such as technological advancements, shifts in consumer behaviour, or changes in the economy?

Target Audience Needs: Based on your consumer research, identify specific problems that your target market is facing. How can your product or service provide a solution that your competitors are not currently offering?

Competitive Advantage: Use your research to develop a strategy that highlights your unique strengths and creates barriers for competitors.

Synthesising the Data for Business Success

The information you gather from your research will be invaluable in deciding whether or not your business idea is worth pursuing. By considering consumer needs, competitive pressures, and market trends, you'll be equipped to make data-driven decisions that set your business up for long-term success.

Key Takeaways:

1. **Refine Your Business Idea**: Use the insights from your research to fine-tune your product or service offering to meet customer needs and stand out in the marketplace.

2. **Validate Demand**: Ensure that there is sufficient demand for your business before making large investments in time and resources.

3. **Identify and Address Market Gaps**: Understand where your competitors are falling short and develop a strategy to fill those gaps with your unique value proposition.

4. **Develop an Actionable Strategy**: Create a clear plan for how you will launch your business based on the research findings, ensuring that you focus on areas with the most potential for success.

Exercise: Research Questions for Deepening Your Understanding

Consumer Research:

1. **Who is your likely consumer base?**

Define the demographics (age, gender, income, education level, etc.) of your ideal customers.

What are their primary pain points that your product/service can address?

2. **What do consumers want?**

What are the most important factors driving their purchasing decisions (price, quality, convenience, brand reputation)?

Are there any evolving trends or shifts in consumer behaviour that could impact your business?

3. **Why will consumers choose your product or service over others?**

What makes your offering compelling? Is it your product's unique features, customer service, convenience, or price?

Competitor Research:

1. **Who are your top 5 competitors?**
List them and analyse their strengths and weaknesses.

2. **How accessible is their business?**
Do they have both physical and online channels? How effective are they in using these channels to reach consumers?

3. **How does their product or service compare to yours?**
What features or qualities do their products have that are similar or different from yours?

4. **What are their strengths and weaknesses?**
Identify areas where competitors excel and where they fall short.

5. **What strategies are they using to attract customers?**
Examine their marketing efforts, customer engagement tactics, and overall branding.

6. **What can you do differently to compete?**
Based on your research, identify how your business can stand out and offer something that competitors do not.

By following these research steps and asking the right questions, you'll be well on your way to launching a business that is informed, strategic, and prepared for success. Research is not a one-time task, it's an ongoing process that will continue to inform and guide your decisions as your business evolves.

NARROWING DOWN YOUR BUSINESS IDEAS
A Strategic Approach

In this section, we'll continue the process of evaluating the business ideas you generated through earlier brainstorming and market scanning exercises. By narrowing down your options, you'll focus your efforts on the concepts with the highest potential for success. To guide you through this process, we will apply a structured **Traffic Light System**, which will help you eliminate less promising ideas and focus on the best ones.

However, narrowing down ideas isn't just about tossing out the less viable ones. It's about honing in on those that fit your skills, passions, market demand, and long-term goals. The deeper you go into this process, the more clarity you'll gain on which idea truly represents the future you envision for yourself.

The Traffic Light System: Your Idea Evaluation Tool

The **Traffic Light System** is a simple, yet powerful tool for categorising and assessing business ideas based on their potential. The system breaks down your ideas into three categories:

1. **NO**: Ideas you will not pursue. These could be discarded for a variety of reasons, such as:

    - Lack of personal interest or passion.
    - Unrealistic or unfeasible in the market.
    - Mismatch with your skills, resources, or expertise.

2. **MAYBE**: Ideas that show some promise but need more investigation. These ideas might require:

    - Additional market research.
    - Skill development.
    - Financial investment or logistical planning.

3. **YES**: Ideas that you are highly excited about and see real potential in. These ideas are:

    - Aligned with your passion, vision, and business goals.
    - Feasible given your available resources.
    - Likely to solve a real customer pain point or fulfil a need in the market.

How to Apply the Traffic Light System: A Step-by-Step Process

Step 1: Create a List of All Your Ideas

Take a moment to list all the business ideas you've brainstormed so far. Don't hold back, write down anything that's come to mind, no matter how vague or ambitious it might seem.

Step 2: Categorise Each Idea

Evaluate each idea and place it under one of the three categories:

NO: Eliminate ideas that feel like dead ends. These are concepts that you're not passionate about, or that simply don't make sense to pursue.

MAYBE: For ideas that seem promising but need more research or development, place them here. These ideas might still require fine-tuning, or you may need to gather more information before moving forward.

YES: For ideas that make your heart race and align with your goals, place them in the "YES" column. These are the ideas that seem worth your time and energy.

Step 3: Reflect on Your Choices

Once you've categorised your ideas, step back and reflect on why you placed each idea in a specific column. Ask yourself:

Why did I place this idea in the "NO" column?

- Does it conflict with my personal goals or values?
- Is it outside of my expertise or capabilities?
- Is the market saturated or unprofitable?

Why did I place this idea in the "MAYBE" column?

- What additional research or resources do I need to make this idea more viable?
- Is there a way to pivot or adapt this idea to make it stronger?

Why did I place this idea in the "YES" column?

- Does it truly excite me?
- Does it solve a clear problem or address a need in the market?
- Do I have the skills, resources, and market access to make it work?

This reflection will help you better understand your decision-making process, and in turn, make your final decision stronger and more confident.

Selecting Your Top Ideas for Further Exploration

Once you've placed your ideas in the **YES** column, it's time to narrow them down even further. Here's how:

1. **Select Two Ideas**: Choose two of your **YES** ideas to dive deeper into. These should be the ones you feel the most excitement about and those that you believe have the most potential for success.

2. **Prioritise Based on Key Criteria**: Before finalising your choice, apply the following filters to help guide your decision:

Passion & Alignment: Which of these ideas are you most passionate about? Passion fuels persistence, and it's a critical driver for success.

Market Demand: Which of these ideas addresses a clear, unmet need in the market? You want an idea with strong demand and long-term sustainability.

Scalability: Which of these ideas has the potential to scale? Consider whether you can expand the business, increase your customer base, and grow your revenue over time.

Beyond the Traffic Light System: Additional Considerations

While the **Traffic Light System** is an excellent tool for organising and evaluating ideas, it's just one part of a broader decision-making process. Here are a few additional elements you should consider when narrowing down your business ideas:

1. **Personal Fit and Skills Assessment**

Do you have the necessary skills to execute this idea? If not, are you willing to learn or partner with someone who does? The best ideas often require a balance of expertise and commitment.

Take an honest inventory of your strengths and weaknesses. Entrepreneurs succeed when they work within their areas of competence or build teams that complement their skills.

2. **Customer Focus: Solving Real Problems**

Ensure your idea solves a real problem or addresses a deep need in your target market. Business success often hinges on the ability to meet customer demands effectively. Is your business idea solving a significant pain point for your ideal customers?

If you haven't already, start conducting preliminary customer interviews or surveys. Listen to potential customers' challenges, frustrations, and needs. This will validate or challenge your assumptions about the market.

3. **Feasibility Check**

Cost of Entry: What are the startup costs involved in each idea? Do you have the financial resources, or will you need outside funding?

Time Commitment: How much time will it take to get each idea off the ground? Are you able to dedicate the required time to make this idea a reality? Be realistic about how much time you can commit to your business and weigh it against your other responsibilities.

4. **Risk and Reward**

Evaluate the potential risks and rewards associated with each idea. Every business venture carries some level of risk, whether it's financial, reputational, or operational. Consider the worst-case scenario and how you can mitigate those risks.

Does the reward justify the risk? Entrepreneurs must weigh the potential upside of their business idea against the resources, time, and risk involved.

5. **Market Validation**

Before fully committing, it's crucial to validate your idea through some form of **proof of concept**. This could be as simple as a landing page, a prototype, or a small-scale test of your service or product. Validation reduces the guesswork and increases your confidence that you're building something customers actually want.

6. **Your Long-Term Vision**

Reflect on how each idea fits into your long-term business vision. Does it have the potential to evolve into something bigger, or does it feel more like a "side hustle"? Will it allow you to achieve your broader business and personal goals?

Exercise: Process of Elimination Table

Here's the updated **Process of Elimination Table**, which helps you filter your ideas further. It's a visual tool that allows you to see your ideas clearly in front of you and make quick decisions based on your evaluations.

Business Idea	NO	MAYBE	YES
Idea 1			✓
Idea 2		✓	
Idea 3	✓		
Idea 4			✓

Conclusion: Moving from Ideas to Action

Now that you've successfully narrowed down your ideas, it's time to dive into a **Viability Assessment** for the top two ideas in your **YES** column. This next stage will help you assess the practicality of each idea and refine it further, taking into account market size, competition, and potential profitability.

The **Traffic Light System** helps you make more structured, objective decisions about which business ideas to pursue. But remember narrowing down ideas is just the first step in your entrepreneurial journey. Stay focused, stay open to new possibilities, and continue refining your ideas until you find the one that truly clicks.

By following this process, you're one step closer to launching a successful business that aligns with your skills, passions, and market opportunities.

Action Plan:

1. **Complete the Traffic Light System**: Review and categorise your business ideas.

2. **Select Your Top 2 Ideas**: Choose two **YES** ideas that you'll pursue further.

3. **Conduct a Viability Assessment**: Dive deeper into these ideas to assess their market potential, profitability, and scalability.

BUSINESS VIABILITY
SWOT Analysis for Entrepreneurs

At this stage, you've narrowed your options down to two strong business ideas. Now, it's time to assess the viability of these ideas to determine which one offers the most potential for success. To do this effectively, we'll utilise a proven business strategy tool: the **SWOT Analysis**.

This powerful tool will help you evaluate both the **internal** and **external** factors affecting your business idea. By examining the **Strengths, Weaknesses, Opportunities**, and **Threats** associated with each business model, you can make an informed decision on which venture to pursue.

What is SWOT Analysis?

SWOT stands for:

- **Strengths**: The internal factors that give your business an edge.
- **Weaknesses**: Internal challenges or areas for improvement.
- **Opportunities**: External factors that could help your business grow.
- **Threats**: External factors that could hinder your progress.

By analysing these four categories, you gain a 360-degree view of your business potential. This will allow you to take decisive action in the areas where you need improvement and capitalise on your strengths and market opportunities.

Step 1: Assess Your Strengths

Strengths are the internal advantages that give your business an edge in the market. These are the unique aspects of your business that can help you deliver value to your customers, beat competitors, and achieve your business goals.

Consider these key areas when evaluating your strengths:

Personal Skills & Expertise: What unique skills, knowledge, or experience do you bring to the table? This can include leadership, technical expertise, or industry-specific experience.

Branding & Positioning: Do you have a strong, memorable brand that resonates with your target market? A compelling value proposition or a unique selling point (USP) can significantly strengthen your business's appeal.

Resources & Assets: What assets do you have access to? This could include financial capital, physical resources (e.g., office space, equipment), or intellectual property (e.g., patents, trademarks).

Networks & Relationships: Who do you know, and who can help you succeed? Your network, whether it's personal or professional, can provide invaluable support, partnerships, and access to customers.

Product or Service Quality: Does your product or service offer a high level of quality or innovation that differentiates you from competitors?

Step 2: Identify Weaknesses

Every business, no matter how promising, has areas that need improvement. Identifying these weaknesses early on is essential so that you can take corrective action before they undermine your success.

Some common weaknesses to consider include:

Lack of Experience or Knowledge: Are you familiar with all the key elements of your industry? A limited understanding of the market, customer behaviour, or your competition can hinder your growth.

Resource Constraints: Do you have adequate resources, both financial and human, to implement your vision? A shortage of capital, lack of manpower, or insufficient infrastructure could be major obstacles.

Inefficient Processes: Are your business processes streamlined and effective? Poor internal systems, disorganised operations, or inadequate customer service processes can impact productivity and customer satisfaction.

Time Management & Motivation: Are you able to focus and prioritise your time effectively? Poor time management or lack of motivation can stall business progress and harm long-term success.

Step 3: Explore Opportunities

Opportunities are external factors that could help your business thrive. They often arise from trends or gaps in the marketplace and recognising them can allow you to expand your market share or even pivot your business model for increased profitability.

Here are some examples of potential opportunities for your business:

Market Gaps: Is there a niche in the market that your business can fill? Identifying and targeting underserved customer segments can give you a competitive advantage.

Industry Trends & Growth Potential: Is your industry experiencing growth or innovation? By staying ahead of trends, you can align your business to capture emerging opportunities.

Access to Funding: Are there grants, loans, or venture capital options available that can provide capital to scale your business?

Partnerships & Collaborations: Could collaborating with other businesses or influencers help you grow? Strategic partnerships can open up new revenue streams and provide access to new customer bases.

Technological Advancements: Is there a new technology that could enhance your product or service? Innovations in tech can improve efficiency, quality, or customer experience.

Global Market Expansion: Can you expand beyond your local market? The rise of online platforms and globalisation has created new opportunities for businesses to reach international customers.

Step 4: Anticipate Threats

The business landscape is full of challenges, and being aware of potential threats is crucial for long-term sustainability. Threats are external factors that could negatively impact your business if not managed effectively.

Common threats to consider include:

Competitive Pressure: Are there strong competitors in your market? A crowded competitive field may require you to adopt innovative strategies to maintain a strong market position.

Market Saturation: Has your market become oversaturated? A high level of competition, combined with low entry barriers, may make it more difficult to differentiate your business.

Economic Factors: Is the economy stable, or are there risks of downturns that could affect your business operations? Economic instability, inflation, or shifts in consumer spending patterns can impact your business's bottom line.

Regulatory Changes: Are there any upcoming changes in laws or regulations that could impact your business? This could include tax reforms, environmental laws, or other government policies that could affect operations, product offerings, or costs.

Technological Disruptions: Could emerging technologies pose a threat to your business? Rapid technological advancements or shifts in consumer behaviour could disrupt traditional business models.

Supply Chain Disruptions: Are you overly reliant on specific suppliers or manufacturers? Supply chain challenges, especially in globalised markets, can impact product availability and pricing.

Case Study: SWOT Analysis for an Online Letting Agency

Let's put this all into perspective with a practical example. Below is a sample SWOT analysis for an **Online Letting Agency**:

Strengths:

Negotiation Skills: Strong ability to close deals and secure profitable contracts.

Industry Experience: Familiarity with the property market and relevant legislation.

Customer-Oriented: Focus on providing excellent customer service and building lasting relationships.

Network: Strong professional contacts within the property and real estate industry.

Weaknesses:

Poor Branding: The business lacks a strong, recognisable brand that resonates with target customers.

Limited Capital: Insufficient financial resources to scale quickly.

Administrative Inefficiencies: Poor time management and administrative skills that slow business operations.

Lack of Manpower: Unable to handle high volumes of business on a solo basis.

Opportunities:

Market Growth: The property rental market is expanding, with increasing demand for online services.

Geographical Expansion: Opportunities to grow beyond local markets into other regions or even internationally.

Commercial Lettings: Potential to diversify services and tap into commercial property leasing or service accommodations.

Technology Integration: Use of property management software to streamline operations and improve customer experience.

Threats:

Intense Competition: A highly competitive market with numerous local and national players.

Economic Downturn: Economic instability or housing market crashes could slow business growth.

Changes in Legislation: Potential changes in property laws, rent controls, or tenant rights could impact the business.

Cash Flow Challenges: Late payments or non-paying tenants could strain financial stability.

Conclusion & Actionable Insights

The SWOT analysis provides you with valuable insights into the viability of your business idea. By thoroughly evaluating each of these four areas, you'll gain clarity on your strengths to leverage, weaknesses to address, opportunities to pursue, and threats to mitigate.

Once you've completed your SWOT analysis for both business ideas, you'll be in a stronger position to make an informed decision on which direction to pursue. It's likely that you'll gravitate toward the business that aligns with your strengths and presents the most promising opportunities.

However, always weigh the risks and rewards, and remember that your business will need ongoing refinement and adaptation to stay competitive and viable. Keep your focus on what will help you sustain long-term growth and success in an ever-changing market.

Next Steps:

- Use the SWOT framework to evaluate the remaining business ideas.

- Identify which business offers the best balance of strengths, opportunities, and manageable risks.

- Develop strategies to address weaknesses and threats as you move forward with your business plan.

Reflective Questions:

As you move forward with your analysis and decision-making process, take a moment to reflect on the following questions:

How did you get on?
Did you feel confident in identifying the strengths, weaknesses, opportunities, and threats for each business? Did anything surprise you about your assessment?

What did you learn about yourself and your business?
Did the SWOT analysis help you identify skills, resources, or areas for improvement that you hadn't fully considered? What insights did you gain about your readiness to pursue either of these ideas?

Have you decided on which business to go with?
Take a moment to assess: which business idea aligns best with your goals, values, and available resources? Why did you make that decision? What specific reasoning guided you to choose one idea over the other?

These questions are designed to help you clarify your thought process and solidify your decision. They also help in assessing whether your choice is based on your strengths and ambitions or if you need to reconsider some aspects before committing fully. The goal is to make an informed decision that will set you up for long-term success and sustainability in your business venture.

Conclusion

The **SWOT analysis** serves as a strategic tool to help you choose the best business idea for you. By answering the reflective questions above, you can deepen your understanding of both the market and yourself. Take your time with this process, as it's essential to ensure you're making the most informed decision possible.

Once you've finalised your choice, you'll be ready to move on to the next phase: creating a strategic plan for your business. This is where you'll define your vision, set actionable goals, and build the framework to turn your entrepreneurial dreams into a thriving business. In Book 3, we'll explore **Strategic and Business Planning** to guide you through this critical stage of your entrepreneurial journey.

THE BUSINESS ENVIRONMENT
P.E.S.T.L.E Analysis

Congratulations!

You've taken an important step toward building your entrepreneurial empire. As you continue on this exciting journey, it's essential to gain a clear understanding of the environment in which your business will operate. The success of any business is influenced not only by its internal capabilities but also by the external factors that shape its environment.

One of the most effective tools for analysing the external factors impacting your business is the **P.E.S.T.L.E.**

Analysis. This acronym stands for:

- Political
- Economical
- Socio-Cultural
- Technological
- Legal
- Environmental

Each of these factors plays a significant role in shaping the way you run your business. Whether you're launching a local startup or planning to scale globally, understanding these external forces will help you make more informed decisions and adapt more effectively.

In this section, we will break down the P.E.S.T.L.E. analysis into its key components, explore their potential impacts on your business, and provide practical guidance for integrating these insights into your strategy.

Political Factors

The political environment can have a profound impact on how your business operates. It refers to the influence that government policies, regulations, and political stability (or instability) have on your business. Understanding the political landscape is crucial to mitigating risks and capitalising on opportunities.

Key considerations include:

Government regulations: How do local, regional, and national laws affect your business? This includes everything from industry-specific regulations to labour laws, taxes, and trade tariffs.

Taxation policies: Consider how tax rates, import/export duties, and government incentives (such as subsidies or grants) might affect your cost structure, profit margins, and competitive positioning.

Trade policies and international relations: If you're doing business internationally, keep an eye on trade agreements, tariffs, and diplomatic relations that could impact your supply chain, market access, and overall business strategy.

As a business owner, staying informed about political shifts allows you to adjust quickly and make strategic decisions that minimise risks, such as moving operations to more politically stable regions or lobbying for policy changes that benefit your industry.

Economic Factors

Economic conditions are among the most critical external factors affecting your business. Whether you're operating in a booming economy or during a recession, economic forces directly influence consumer behaviour, business costs, and growth potential.

Key areas to assess include:

Inflation and interest rates: These can directly impact the cost of borrowing, consumer purchasing power, and overall demand for your product or service.

Disposable income: If consumers have more disposable income, they may be willing to spend more on your product. Conversely, during economic downturns, consumer spending may decrease.

Capital availability: The ability to secure funding, whether through loans, investors, or grants, depends largely on the economic climate. A tight credit market can limit your growth potential, whereas favourable interest rates and investor confidence can open doors to capital.

Recession and unemployment: A high unemployment rate or an economic recession can influence consumer demand and your workforce's productivity. Understanding these dynamics helps you position your business strategically in tougher times.

In turbulent economic conditions, it's essential to be agile. Have contingency plans in place to pivot your business model or product offering to better meet market needs. For instance, if you're launching a luxury product during a recession, consider creating more affordable variations.

Socio-Cultural Factors

Understanding socio-cultural trends is vital for aligning your business with the needs and values of your target market. These factors influence consumer behaviour, preferences, and lifestyle choices, all of which impact demand for your products or services.

Key socio-cultural factors include:

Demographics: Analyse the age, gender, cultural background, income levels, and education of your target market. These factors can help you tailor your marketing and product offerings to appeal to specific segments.

Lifestyle changes: Shifts in consumer preferences, such as increasing demand for sustainable products or digital services, can present new opportunities or challenges for your business.

Social trends and values: Stay aware of shifting social norms and values, such as growing concerns about health and wellness, environmental sustainability, or social justice. Being attuned to these movements can help you position your brand as relevant and aligned with the values of your target audience.

Understanding these socio-cultural factors allows you to anticipate changes in consumer behaviour and adjust your product development, marketing strategies, and customer service approaches accordingly.

Technological Factors

In today's fast-paced business landscape, technological advancements are a key driver of growth, efficiency, and innovation. Staying ahead of the technology curve can significantly enhance your competitive edge.

Technological factors to consider include:

Digital tools and automation: Leveraging software, apps, and AI to streamline operations, reduce costs, and improve customer experiences is crucial. Think about automating administrative tasks or using digital marketing to enhance your brand's reach.

Online presence and e-commerce: With increasing numbers of consumers shopping online, having an effective digital strategy (including a website, social media, and e-commerce platform) is essential for business growth.

Innovation and R&D: Stay innovative by adopting cutting-edge technologies that can enhance your products, services, or customer experience. This could range from incorporating AI into customer service to using blockchain for secure transactions.

Failing to keep up with technological advancements can lead to falling behind competitors who are better positioned to exploit new technologies.

Legal Factors

Understanding the legal landscape in which your business operates is fundamental to avoiding legal pitfalls and ensuring compliance with relevant laws. Violations can result in hefty fines, reputational damage, or even business closure.

Key legal considerations include:

Business licenses and permits: Ensure that you are fully licensed to operate in your industry and geographic location. This could include federal, state, or local permits.

Consumer protection laws: These laws safeguard consumers against fraud, unfair practices, and poor-quality products. You must ensure that your business adheres to consumer rights laws regarding refunds, warranties, and dispute resolution.

Intellectual property protection: If your business involves proprietary technology or creative assets, securing trademarks, copyrights, and patents is crucial to protecting your intellectual property from infringement.

Employment law: If you employ staff, you must comply with labour laws governing wages, working hours, employee rights, and health and safety regulations.

Failure to comply with legal regulations can result in lawsuits, penalties, and loss of credibility in the market.

Environmental Factors

In an increasingly environmentally conscious world, businesses must consider their impact on the planet. Environmental sustainability is not just a social responsibility but often a competitive advantage.

Environmental considerations include:

Climate change: Be aware of how environmental shifts, such as extreme weather patterns or rising sea levels, could impact your business. This is especially important for businesses in agriculture, logistics, and tourism.

Waste management and sustainability: Consider how your business can reduce its carbon footprint and minimise waste. Implementing eco-friendly practices can improve your brand image and reduce operational costs in the long run.

Environmental regulations: Governments are increasingly enacting stricter environmental laws. Stay ahead by adopting green business practices and ensuring compliance with local environmental laws.

Even if your business isn't directly related to environmental industries, demonstrating corporate social responsibility (CSR) through eco-friendly initiatives can attract more customers and enhance your reputation.

Putting It All Together: Analysing Your Business Environment

By systematically analysing each of these factors through a P.E.S.T.L.E. lens, you'll gain a comprehensive understanding of the environment in which your business operates. Below is an example of how a P.E.S.T.L.E. analysis might look for a business.

Example: P.E.S.T.L.E. Analysis for an Online Letting Agency

Political: Local rental regulations, tenant protection laws, and tax policies related to rental income.

Economic: Market rental rates, the affordability of tenants, and the impact of interest rates on property investments.

Socio-Cultural: Demographics of renters, changing preferences for renting versus owning, and attitudes toward sustainable housing.

Technological: Use of property management software, virtual tours for listings, and online payment systems.

Legal: Landlord responsibilities, tenant rights, and real estate laws.

Environmental: Impact of climate change on property values and the importance of sustainable buildings.

Exercise: Conduct Your Own P.E.S.T.L.E. Analysis

Now, take some time to apply the P.E.S.T.L.E. analysis framework to your own business idea. Use the blank template provided to map out how each factor may influence your operations. Reflect on how these insights could inform your business strategy and decision-making.

Political	
Economical	
Social	
Technological	
Legal	
Enviornmental	

Reflective Questions:

1. How did you find the P.E.S.T.L.E. analysis process?

2. What key insights did you uncover about your business environment?

3. How will these insights influence the way you plan and operate your business?

4. How can you continuously monitor and adapt to external factors affecting your business?

Regularly revisiting your P.E.S.T.L.E. analysis will ensure that you stay responsive to external changes, capitalise on emerging opportunities, and mitigate potential risks. By keeping a pulse on these environmental factors, you can position your business for long-term success and sustainability.

Conclusion:

The P.E.S.T.L.E. analysis is not a one-time exercise; it's a dynamic tool that should evolve as your business grows and the external environment changes. By staying proactive and informed, you can navigate uncertainties, identify new opportunities, and position your business for lasting success in a competitive marketplace.

FINAL THOUGHTS & ADDITIONAL INFORMATION

Congratulations! You've now laid the groundwork for your entrepreneurial journey by identifying a viable business idea. But having a solid business idea is just the beginning. To transform your idea into a successful venture, you need a well-defined action plan, something that will guide your decisions, keep you focused, and allow you to navigate the inevitable challenges that come with running your own business.

As you move forward, consider this a pivotal moment. You have the knowledge and the tools to build your business, but the next step is critical: translating this knowledge into action. This means creating a strategic roadmap that will help you achieve your goals, make informed decisions, and continually assess your progress.

In this closing section, we'll touch on some essential concepts and additional insights that will help you move from idea to implementation, including a brief recap of key topics we've covered:

The Nature of an Entrepreneur

Being an entrepreneur is not just about starting a business; it's about adopting a mindset. It's a way of thinking that is innovative, driven, and resilient. Successful entrepreneurs are problem-solvers who thrive in uncertainty, are comfortable with risk, and are determined to turn their ideas into reality. The path of entrepreneurship is not always easy, but it's one that requires grit, creativity, and adaptability. By now, you should have a clearer understanding of what it takes to succeed in this dynamic role.

Motives Fuelling Aspirations

As you reflect on your entrepreneurial journey, consider what fuels your drive. Motivation is often rooted in personal goals, whether it's financial independence, the desire for flexibility, or a passion to solve a particular problem in society. Your motives will influence your business decisions and shape the way you approach obstacles. Understanding your 'why' will help you stay grounded when things get tough, and it will inspire you to keep moving forward.

How to Generate Business Ideas: A Comprehensive Approach for Entrepreneurs

One of the most important skills for an entrepreneur is the ability to identify new opportunities. In this book, we've outlined practical approaches for generating innovative business ideas, whether by spotting gaps in the market, leveraging your expertise, or simply looking for ways to improve existing products and services. A good business idea doesn't have to be revolutionary; sometimes, it's about making small improvements that meet the needs of your target audience.

The Research Process: Laying the Foundation for a Successful Business

Research is the bedrock of any successful business. Understanding your market, industry trends, competitors, and customer needs is essential for making informed decisions. In this book, we've explored the importance of conducting thorough research to help you identify business opportunities, evaluate your competition, and understand the landscape in which your business will operate. The more data you gather, the better equipped you'll be to make strategic choices.

Narrowing Down Your Business Ideas: A Strategic Approach

With a pool of ideas at your disposal, the next step is narrowing them down to the one with the highest potential. This involves carefully analysing each idea based on your research, resources, and personal strengths. Remember, not all business ideas are created equal, and some will have more potential for scalability, profitability, and sustainability than others. This step will help you focus your energy and resources on what truly matters.

Business Viability: SWOT Analysis for Entrepreneurs

Understanding whether your business idea is viable is crucial for ensuring long-term success. The SWOT analysis (Strengths, Weaknesses, Opportunities, and Threats) offers a structured way to assess your business concept. By identifying your internal strengths and weaknesses and evaluating external opportunities and threats, you can better position yourself to mitigate risks and capitalise on your strengths.

The Business Environment: P.E.S.T.L.E Analysis

In addition to internal analysis, it's essential to understand the external environment. The PESTLE analysis, focusing on Political, Economic, Social, Technological, Legal, and Environmental factors, helps entrepreneurs identify macro-level influences that could affect their business. By staying ahead of these trends, you can anticipate challenges, identify new opportunities, and make smarter business decisions.

Moving Forward: Creating an Action Plan

With the foundations set, the next step is to create a clear action plan for moving forward. This involves setting specific, measurable, and time-bound goals that will guide the growth of your business. Identify key milestones, assess your resources, and develop strategies to overcome potential obstacles. Remember, an action plan isn't static, it should evolve as your business grows and adapts to new opportunities and challenges.

Additional Resources for Entrepreneurs

Starting and growing a business is a journey that requires continuous learning, innovation, and perseverance. For many of you, the next natural question might be: "How do I kick-start my business?" This is where the next books in the *Becoming Your Own Boss* series come in.

Book 2 - NO TIME FOR EXCUSES:

If you've ever found yourself making excuses, whether it's about lack of time, money, or resources, this book is for you. It will help you turn those negative self-talks into positive actions. Excuses often hold aspiring entrepreneurs back, but with the right mindset and strategies, you can overcome these barriers and start taking concrete steps toward launching your business.

This book offers proven systems and strategies to help you move forward, regardless of the hurdles you may face.

Book 3 - STRATEGIC PLAN & BUSINESS PLAN:

In this book, I'll guide you through the critical process of drafting a vision and mission statement, setting clear business goals, and developing a robust strategy. You'll also gain practical insights on writing a business plan, a fundamental document that outlines your business model, market research, operational plan, financial projections, and growth strategy.

This book is designed to provide a blueprint that will help you attract investors, secure funding, and set your business on the path to success.

Staying Connected

Starting a business can be an isolating experience, and sometimes you'll need advice, motivation, or just someone to share your successes and struggles with. If you've found the information in this book valuable, I encourage you to reach out. Whether you have questions, need additional resources, or simply want to share your progress, I'd love to hear from you. Feel free to contact me at riverflowwriters@hotmail.co.uk.

Final Words of Encouragement

The entrepreneurial journey is unique for everyone, but it's always filled with opportunities for growth, learning, and success. It may not always be easy, but the rewards of building something from the ground up are incredibly fulfilling. Keep pushing forward, stay focused, and never stop learning. You have the potential to achieve great things, and I'm excited to see where your entrepreneurial spirit will take you.

Best of luck and may your business journey be nothing short of extraordinary.

Maxine J. Lovell

www.ingramcontent.com/pod-product-compliance
Lightning Source LLC
Chambersburg PA
CBHW070455220526
45466CB00004B/1834